SILVER PLATTER SERVICE

How to Create a Culture of Excellence

SILVER PLATTER SERVICE

How to Create a Culture of Excellence

Randy Fox

FoxPoint LLC
P.O. Box 676, Oxford, FL 34484

Silver Platter Service: How To Create A Culture Of Excellence

ISBN 978-0-9914669-5-5 (Paperback)

Cover design: Irish Eyes Design, Aurelie Gallagher

Interior Design: Trevor Fox, https://www.trevorjamesfox.com/

Interior Images: Courtesy of Randy Fox, unless otherwise noted

Printed in the United States of America

First Printing, 2020

For my favorite team, my family.

TABLE OF CONTENTS

SECTION ONE | THE AGENTS OF CHANGE

SECTION TWO | THE TRUST FACTOR

SECTION THREE | BRINGING EVERYONE TOGETHER

FOREWORD

The phrase silver platter service instantly brings to mind excellence, the highest levels of quality, the best.

Any time we commit to such excellence, we know that there will be significant effort. You see, it is easy to make the commitment to excellence. Living that commitment daily is difficult. Anyone can say, "We're committed to excellence." Few will follow that statement with disciplined thinking and action. However, that is exactly what we should do, and it is exactly what this book helps us do.

In this helpful book, Randy Fox calls us to excellence and shows us how to achieve it by example and precept. Having served and led organizations of various sizes and types, I find Randy's ideas both classic and fresh. Even those of us who have been thinking about, reading on, and pursuing the importance of change, trust, and working effectively together will find fresh ideas and examples here, all of which can be adapted to numerous other situations.

What is worthwhile is worth working for. That is certainly true as we pursue our mission with the qualities Randy lays out. Ultimately, leadership is about people – as reminded here, "People Matter Most."

As you journey through these pages, I am confident that you will be challenged, encouraged, and inspired. And, ultimately, you too can create the culture within your organization that you most deeply desire. As you do, others will look at your organization and know there is something different and special going on because of the Silver Platter Service they experience.

Samuel W. "Dub" Oliver, Ph.D.
President, Union University

PROLOGUE

After years of traveling the country speaking to leaders, teams, and organizations – including corporations, small businesses, school districts, and nonprofits – there's one thing I have found they all have in common:

They are all interested in performing well as a team, at the very highest level.

Nearly every person and team I've worked with is interested in working in a culture of excellence. People want to be a part of something that serves well, produces great results, and achieves at the highest level.

I'm sure if you and I were face to face right now, you would say you want this for your team too!

Let's be clear, when I say "team" I'm not just speaking about a sports situation.

We are talking about the teams that you do life with; from your family to your work team to your neighborhood and community in which you live.

In all of these environments, you, more than likely, want to work and associate with others who have a real passion to collaborate, to be respected, and ultimately achieve goals that make a difference.

You want to bring value, and know that your team does as well.

As we begin our journey, we have to be prepared to ask and answer some really difficult questions.

What does it take to have a team culture that is truly growing, transforming and achieving results?

What does it look like for a team to truly work effectively and efficiently together?

What steps and strategies are necessary and vital to have a high-performing team?

How do you go about delivering the best service - silver platter level service - in everything that your team does?

How do you instill excellence in service?

How do you practically engage everyone on the team so they are performing at their individual best?

What does it take to create this type of high

performing team, bonded together in a culture destined for success?

In summary, how does a group of different people, with different backgrounds, ideas, family structure, education, and so on, come together to consistently work as a unit to accomplish common goals?

Wow, lots of tough questions, and even harder work to answer them with consistently positive results.

One of the foundational elements to these answers is discovered in one word. The word ingrained in this book.

Culture.

Yes, your team does have a culture.

Whether you like it or not, whether you even know what it is, every organization has one. Your family has one. Your church has one.

Every gathering of people creates a culture.

Your culture is a combination of values, goals, activities, priorities, characteristics, attitudes, and much more.

It is developed over time, based on who is in the organization or team, what you focus on, how you live, and how you work on a daily basis. Culture will be the foundation of your success or the breakdown of your organization.

I know you want success.

You want to be part of a team culture that serves, grows, and brings value to the world. Your organization has purpose and by fulfilling it, you will reap a piece of that joy as well.

Now let's be clear and say this again, every team has a culture. This book is about creating the one you want and need.

We will review, study, and share how to create a culture and transform a team so your performance levels are high, employees are highly engaged, and success isn't just a dream, it's a daily reality.

This book is separated into 3 elements, they are:

- » The Agents of Change
- » The Trust Factor
- » Bringing Everyone Together

You will discover easy, actionable insights and examples that you can apply to your team to increase your service levels.

The first key is the decision it takes to start. You have to be intentional to simply change. Then, you must have solid, repeated steps focused on increasing trust. Finally, there are the necessary ongoing actions that can easily sustain you to your destination by bringing everyone together.

This is the type of culture transformation which will

improve excellence in your team and is exactly what produces better results. Furthermore, it brings about lasting engagement with employees and ongoing satisfaction from clients.

The focus here is not on the end result. The focus is on the process of having the right culture in place that will take you, and keep you, where you want to be.

A destination of silver platter service!

This is going to be a fast, amazing and transformational journey!

Are you ready?

THE AGENTS OF CHANGE

section one

chapter one

CLOSE THE GAP

I'm sure you can think of a variety of great reasons why it matters to have a team with a culture of excellence and high levels of service.

If you need some help, here's proof.

In April of 2020, our team at FoxPoint conducted a national survey of hundreds of working adults. I will refer to this survey several times throughout the book.

A key data point was based on customer service levels. In our society today, we all work with and receive services and products, from a variety of organizations.

We asked about general service levels in our society with providers of all types.

On a scale of 1 to 100, with 1 being poor and 100

being fabulous (the absolute best), we asked people to rate the service levels they received.

The compiled score was a pathetic, yet not surprising, 60.

Sixty.

Way below acceptable!

You know what that means; there is a massive perceived service gap.

That gap, a gap of 40 points, is a potential 67% increase in opportunity.

How much would your organization, team, business, school, non-profit (you name it) thrive, grow, and achieve if you could close that gap?

For a business, what would it mean if you could increase customer satisfaction by 67%?

For educators, what does it mean to have parents, students, and your community more satisfied with your service?

This just scratches the surface of service and the impact to organizations.

When service levels are perceived to be down, so is morale, so is employee engagement, so is everything in the operation.

Here is the brutal truth. You cannot afford that

perception to be your reality. You have to close the gap.

You have to create a culture of excellence.

Now.

And it begins with a decision.

A decision you may not want to make. There may even be fear and resistance as a result.

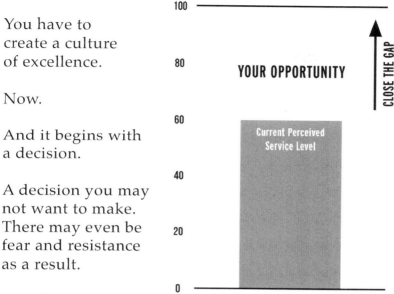

See, this decision will take you into potentially uncharted terrority.

Yet, that is exactly what you must do in order to create the type of culture you desire.

Regardless, the fact you are still reading speaks to the fact that you want it.

You know the work will be hard, but it is necessary. It is just that important.

Why?

Something worth having is something worth fighting for.

Something worth having is something worth fighting for.

LET'S GO!!!

Again I ask, are you ready?

Oh okay, that time I heard you.

chapter two

THE AGENT

As just noted, culture transformation starts with a key element. A decision.

Really, a word.

It is a word that is simple to say, yet complex and completely transforming just by its nature.

Change.

There, I said it. That dreaded word that so many people run from instead of running toward.

Change.

This change process is key to your journey to clearly identify the principles necessary for culture creation and team transformation.

Notice how the words *creation* and *transformation*

immediately tell us that there is going to be change.
Things cannot stay the way they are if we are *creating*
a culture. Things cannot stay the way they are if we
are going through a process of *transformation*.

Change.

You and your team have to be willing to change.

From our study, one thing jumps out in the data
for sure.

We aren't good at change.

Overwhelmingly – nearly double the other seven
categories listed – the ability to identify and adapt
to change is the number ONE area in which teams
struggle. To go deeper, it was selected first by nearly
30% of the respondents.

Let that sink in for a minute. Change is the number
one concern *and* area of struggle for most teams.

If change is the top area of struggle and the gap of
service excellence is so large, no wonder
organizations have a hard time closing the gap!

It can be done.

"Can do" and "will do" are far apart for some
however.

Only the very best will take this step.

Only the very best teams, the very best businesses,

the very best school districts, the very best families, and the very best leaders will take this journey.

I know you *want* to be the best.

The question is, what are you willing to do in pursuit of that excellence?

Let's be clear right now.

This isn't going to be easy.

But, it is so worth it!

As you read the real stories throughout this book, you will discover that the pursuit of excellence is not only worth it, it is necessary.

This pursuit increases employee morale, employee engagement, client satisfaction and bottom line results. It will increase loyalty, build trust, and help your team become a market leader.

Not only will this be hard, the road will be long. In the end, however, it will be well worth it. Sometimes, it may seem like you have been working toward the pursuit of excellence forever.

The only thing that will get you through will be, as my friend Jeff Cross says, "Tenacity and grit." You and your team must persevere.

There can be no quitting.

There can only be persistence.

There must be no negativity.

Only the common belief by each person that you must stay the course.

Persistence. Persistence. Persistence.

Think of your culture creation like building a structure.

Your team, like an architectural and contracting group, is setting out to create something amazing. And just like you, they didn't give up.

Did you know the White House took thirteen years to complete and the Vatican took 144 years to build? Chichen Itza in Mexico, built by the Mayans, was a 400-year venture and the Great Wall of China was a multi-generational project lasting 2,000 years.

Amazing statistics which demonstrate an inspiring truth.

See, in order to create a culture of excellence, you and everyone on your team must be willing to *stay the course*. In our culture of instant gratification, this can be tough.

And, part of that course – many parts actually – will involve change.

Change is something that really can bring out some of the hardest and darkest parts in each of us.

Our world is so upside down right now, and not

functioning as normal. A large part of this book was written during the COVID-19 pandemic crisis.

To say the least, this was certainly a difficult time for everyone.

For the essential workers who had to be on the front lines, things changed. Some of their changes were dramatic and dangerous too. And we are grateful for what they did, how they served us through the changes they made. Thank you for being heroes! Thank you for putting yourselves on the line for others!

Thank you for delivering silver platter service to the world!

For those of us who were considered "non-essential" (like me), things changed too. We stayed home, most of us didn't have our regular routine.

Kids homeschooled, parents did house projects, some were bored, and others worried about income. That brings up an interesting side question; aren't all jobs that provide for our families considered essential? I guess that's a topic for another book.

Either way, these changes brought about anxiety for most.

One thing we heard over and over though is so true: we will get through this...together.

That is what a culture of excellence is about. Not going alone and working well together.

Back to our survey.

The data showed that nearly 50% of us are either hesitant when it comes to change or we hate it.

Wow!

Think of that now in terms of your team.

Based on our survey, it is more than likely that half of your team is not ready to embrace change. How do you progress and create a culture of excellence with that much resistance?

Nearly 50% of us are either hesitant when it comes to change or we hate it.

That is something we simply cannot ignore.

Again, we have to hit change head on and learn the best strategies to help our teams progress together for a sustained journey of excellence.

As we dive deeper, let's break apart the common players when it comes to change. I've found that people typically fall into one of three categories. I call them:

> » The Resistor
> » The Hesitator
> » The Change Agent

Let's take a look at each of them...

chapter three

THE RESISTOR

Like the name says, they flat out resist. Literally everything and anything that isn't comfortable and typical in their routine is denied. They despise change. They never want to adjust, adapt or move. They would rather keep things the way they are than try something new, even if those current things aren't working.

The *Resistors* can kill teams. They can kill progress.

You know these people, and you may (if you're honest) even be one.

Now, this doesn't mean they are bad people. Actually, on the contrary, they tend to be very loyal. They know their jobs and schedules inside and out. They can function very well with routine and accomplish plenty.

They can be steady.

However, when it comes to change, many times there seems to be something or someone to complain about. Negativity tends to surround them; therefore infiltrating the team and the culture.

Any idea is immediately questioned, or shut down.

Maybe you have people in your team that remind you of the *Resistor*.

Now, I get it. Change isn't easy, yet, the ability to adapt, grow and innovate is critical.

Take technology as one example. Try to eliminate the use of technology from your life. It's everywhere, and for the most part, it's good.

Because of the changes over the last 10 to 20 years, we are able to communicate with people through apps, software platforms, text messages and more.

It is so cool to see my 8-year-old daughter online chatting with friends in Illinois, family in Wisconsin and California, and others right here in Florida during COVID-19. In this time of anxiety, changes made previously are making an impact today.

Speaking of the crisis, how about the changes organizations all across the country have made!

Within a couple of weeks, companies made great changes and started making personal protective equipment instead of their normal products. Without their willingness to change, immediately, lives were literally at stake.

In the end, even with *Resistors* at every turn, leaders around the U.S. were forced to make changes. Your local Mayor, your supermarket, your hair stylist, and even restaurants had to make changes.

You had to make changes.

No matter what some of them did or said – and we know they made mistakes, we all do – it seemed there was someone criticizing. There was someone wanting things to remain the same or just have it their way.

There was always someone *resisting*.

Being a *Resistor* can hurt progress, people, your vision, the team, and it squashes results.

Resisting change that can bring about progress is actually resisting the team.

Resisting change that can protect and help people isn't silver platter service.

The team always comes first.

Unfortunately, without proper guidance, *Resistors* may end up putting themselves before the team.

And to be clear, the team always comes first.

You cannot afford to ignore *Resistors*, nor allow them to continue to resist. As we will unpack later, you have to help them navigate the changes.

We will talk more about change agents. For now,

I'm thankful for people who are willing to change. Thankful for people willing to run into the fire, or into the storm, and face the issue head on, even when they don't know what lies ahead.

chapter four

THE HESITATOR

First of all, this is a very large group of people - over 45% based on our survey.

These team members are anxious to speak about what is wrong. They tend to be concerned about things, yet aren't sure what to do about them.

They are open to new ideas, although hesitant to how it will all play out. Thus the name, *Hesitators*.

They may be open to change, but they aren't jumping up and down with joy for another change to come their way. They are curious, yet hesitant; therefore, questioning and processing things methodically before they embrace the newness.

It was the fall of 1999, and while we were all preparing for Y2K to crash our world – which never happened – I was being relocated by my company. At the time, I worked for the fourth largest printing company in the United States, with thousands of employees and 55 manufacturing locations.

After years of learning, growing, failing, and developing as a leader, I was being promoted to Plant Manager. My role was to lead a team of nearly 200 employees, manage the $35 million dollar manufacturing operation, and – oh yeah – turn it around.

There had been issues with service level performance.

Everything from missing delivery dates, to poor quality, to even worse customer service interaction. All of this, as one would expect, was beginning to hurt the reputation, frustrate both internal and external clients, and impact the bottom line.

This subpar level of excellence was not acceptable and senior management was looking for – you guessed it – change!

My first days and weeks in my new role were spent mostly meeting people, asking questions, observing and simply listening. There was a new process of printing for me to learn, as well as a new set of products and services. I needed to learn as much as possible, and fast.

I'll never forget how time after time, as I would pose the question, "Can you explain to me why we do it that way?" I would typically receive the same answer "We've always done it that way."

My follow up questions would be, "Does it work?

Is there a better way?"

You know, for the most part, this group didn't know why they did something the way they did. It was apparent the status quo had taken over. Keeping things the way they were was easier. It was simple, it didn't rock the boat for all of the *Hesitators*.

Sound familiar?

You may know something isn't working, yet the thought of another new thing, or new process forcing additional meetings is more than you can stomach.

We like things to remain comfortable.

We like to know what is expected.

We feel better when routine dominates.

Change means new processes, which means different routines, which means harder work and potentially longer hours.

In reality, though, without asking the tough questions, we don't find the best answers.

In reality, though, without asking the tough questions, we don't find the best answers.

We need to keep asking those tough questions.

Don't let your hesitancy, or the *Hesitators*, keep the status quo just for comfort's sake.

Always yearn for the best.

Always search for changes that are necessary, meaningful, and appropriate to create transformation. This is how you get the team going in the right direction.

I did it in that team, and you need to do it in yours.

How do we move beyond the status quo?

Great question, keep reading for the answers.

chapter five

THE CHANGE AGENT

You may be familiar with an ancient story, a piece of history from the Bible. Even if you aren't, the story is a great example for business leaders, teams and people facing fears in route to becoming
Change Agents.

This goes back literally thousands of years and you may have learned the end of it as a church song when you were a kid.

"Joshua fought the battle of Jericho, Jericho, Jericho. Joshua fought the battle of Jericho and the walls came tumbling down."

If you didn't grow up in church, nor are familiar with the story, no worries. This is still a great example and you will glean knowledge from it to take your team to a higher level.

The story actually begins forty years before the walls

came tumbling down. God had set aside land for the people of Israel to go into and live. It was a land flowing with milk and honey.

It was abundant.

It was the BEST.

Moses (you know, the deliverer of the *10 Commandments*) was leading the people of Israel, and God instructed him to scout out land so they would know where they were headed and what they might face. So, Moses sent twelve men, one from each of the twelve tribes, to check out the land of Canaan.

These men were charged with seeing if the land was full of good food and rich soil. He asked them to find out what type of people were there and how many. If there were trees with fruit, he told them to do their best to bring some back.

Off on their expedition the men went. They found some wonderful things.

They cut off one cluster of grapes to bring back home.

Now, this isn't any cluster you'd pick up at the grocery store. This one cluster was so big they placed it over a very large branch and it took two men to lift and carry it over their shoulders.

This was one serious amount of fruit!

In the end, they found the land to be full of food. It

was beautiful and it would be an amazing place to live.

There was one problem, though. There were well-fortified cities, large walls, and some very large people.

Upon the return of the twelve scouts to Moses, most of the men (ten, to be exact) were somewhere between *Hesitator* and *Resistor*. Some said, "We can't attack them; they are stronger than us....we felt like grasshoppers, and we looked like grasshoppers to them!"

Yet there were two. Two men that knew taking this land was the right thing to do. Two men that said, despite the doubts and the challenges, this land is worth it.

These two men understood that the desert where they were living in slavery, was far worse than the potential greatness that lie ahead in this new land.

They knew a change was necessary.

Still, many of the people fell in line with the ten men speaking the loudest. They were both hesitant and resistant. To the point of even saying, "We should choose a leader and go back to Egypt."

For emphasis, let me reiterate, these people had been *slaves* in Egypt. Why would they want to go back?

See, not knowing what was ahead made them

hesitant. They were reacting and working from a place of fear.

Fear of the unknown.

Fear of others.

Fear of hard work.

Fear of something new.

Fear of fear itself.

The two men that were *The Change Agents*, were Caleb and Joshua.

This is what they had to say, "The land we passed through and explored is exceedingly good. If the Lord is pleased with us, he will lead us into that land, a land flowing with milk and honey, and will give it to us. Only do not rebel against the Lord. And do not be afraid of the people of the land, because we will devour them. Their protection is gone, but the Lord is with us. Do not be afraid of them."
Numbers 14:7-9 NIV

It is amazing when someone leads with courage and a strong belief in the possibilities that change will bring; great progress can take place.

So can great results!

Their confidence in their ability to conquer the land is inspiring.

Unfortunately, if you know the story, the people didn't listen. They were consumed with fear.

They decided it was better to be stuck in their known misery than it would be to try something new. Their desire to keep the known was greater than their motivation to gain something unknown.

This did not sit well with God.

Because they did not listen, God promised to Moses, and to all the people of Israel, that none of them will ever see the land. They will never rejoice in the blessing. They will not achieve their intended best, their purpose, their desired team outcome.

That is, except for two. Yep, Joshua and Caleb.

For 40 years the people stumbled around in the wilderness. They kept on working, eating, and living.

They survived but they didn't thrive.

This, unfortunately, is the fate of many teams in our world today.

And I don't want it to be the fate of your team.

In so many of our teams, people come to work, they stumble around the desert, they do some tasks, they grumble and although something is being done, it isn't the best.

Quite frankly, it isn't even close to their best.

This downward slide results in team members who aren't happy or engaged. The best is sacrificed for mediocre. The *Hesitators* succeed in sharing their fears and prompting the *Resistors* to speak up.

Now, this may not seem like your present team, but every team struggles at times to keep everyone excited about the future.

We have periods of time when things seem stuck.

Service levels drop.

Results tend to follow.

As stuck people tend to do, they gossip.

Gossip leads to secrets and stifled communication.

Trust erodes.

And without trust the whole system collapses.

The list goes on... and so does the story.

When Moses and all of the people that refused to change had died, God opened the land. Joshua (one of the two *Change Agents*) leads the people across the Jordan River.

They arrive and take the land!

It is flowing with milk and honey. It is a wonderful place. The place they were always intended to be. It took 40 years, lots of casualties, but they made it.

Oh, and yes, there is a battle and Joshua fights it by marching his people and blasting trumpets. And you know what? The walls came tumbling down!

This can be the reality for your team too.

Truly.

How?

Keep the motivation for gaining something new and unknown greater than the fear of losing something known.

This story is such a great example of how *The Change Agents* and teams built with that mindset are able to take the promised land.

I'm urging you not to wait forty years to experience it.

Let's make the changes now.

Need help making those changes?

Keep the motivation for gaining something new and unknown greater than the fear of losing something known.

Up next is how to navigate change.

chapter six

HOW TO NAVIGATE CHANGE

After speaking to thousands of people around the country on a variety of team and leadership topics, including change, I've discovered a common thread.

Change is hard.

Here are the most repeated elements I hear as to why change is so hard:

- » Fear of the unknown is uncomfortable
- » Change means I have to give something up
- » Concern over lack of resources
- » Loss of control
- » Lack of buy-in from the team

To address these five very common, and

understandable, reactions (fears), here are some ways you can help your team successfully navigate change (with confidence):

1. Be clear as to the *why* and purpose of the change.

This communication must be consistent, transparent, and repeated. Without information there is no understanding. Without understanding there is fear. With fear there is no change.

With clear communication the direction is received and can be believed.

With clear communication the direction is received and can be believed. With that consistent updating, fear subsides because the unknown is shared and becomes known.

2. Show the positive results that will be achieved.

What is the expected positive outcome from the change? By knowing what the destination is for the changes, people will better understand the outcomes and purposes for them. In addition to the positive outcome, describe what the *positive gain* will be.

True, sometimes we give something up in the process of change. The other truth, though, is that there is something positive to gain in the journey itself. That positive outcome goes back to the *why*, which fuels the reasoning.

The positive outcome will help people on your team

be more focused on what everyone will gain versus what they might lose.

3. Provide the proper resources for your team.

Resources are already scarce enough, and when changing processes creates more work, stress mounts. Will your team have the time, the funding, the technology and most importantly, the leadership resources to navigate the change?

You may need to clear someone's plate and have them be the owner/driver for a major change. I've seen very successful teams work through a year-long technology overhaul. They appointed a single captain for the process. That person steered the discussion, strategy planning, training, and implementation, for every part of the project. This was their *only* job for one year.

You have to decide to dedicate the resources necessary to complete the change.

In the end, tell your people what you will do, do it, and tell them that you are committed to seeing it through to completion.

4. Be honest.

Let's face it, not everyone gets a vote on most changes. The loss of control creates anxiety, distrust, and frustration.

Honestly, change is going to be difficult. However, by following the previous three steps, your team can get through change with less pain.

By acknowledging that change is hard, you are indicating that you understand they may not *want* to do it and you appreciate their willingness to go through it anyway. This is about team leadership building trust and saying, "We get it, and we need you to trust us that we will be better off with these changes in the end."

In the next section of the book, we will focus on trust, because in the end, trust is a huge factor in making changes. In order for your team to move forward with a new vision and accept something that is out of their control, they need to trust you and one another.

5. Make sure you have the right people and spend time with them.

If you have any doubts about your team as you head into your culture creation and pursuit of excellence, this is the time to draw the line. It will be extremely difficult to move forward with people who have negative attitudes, poor performance, or substandard character.

Help them move on. They belong somewhere, but not on your team. There are ways to help them land softly elsewhere. It is very important that you have the right people that you trust, love, and believe in for this journey to be successful.

Now that you have the team you want, be present to encourage them. A changing dynamic requires strong relationships, which requires time spent together.

Intentionally carve out time to:

> » Meet with people; you have to care enough to spend time with them
> » Listen; simply listen to them, hear them out show them empathy
> » Engage; involve them in decision-making and brainstorming as often as possible
> » Be relational; be real and transparent, find out who they are outside of work and what and who matters to them

In the end, navigating change takes time, intentionality, and a focus on people. It takes the best people, working effectively together, pursuing a common goal, to be successful. It takes amazing communicators willing to repeatedly share the *why*.

By understanding, addressing, and approaching change as something that brings your team to a brighter future, you will succeed.

THE TRUST FACTOR

section two

chapter seven

THE FACTOR

As we conducted our survey I expected trust to be a key component, yet even I was surprised how overwhelmingly significant it is for people.

Respondents made it very clear, trust is not only important, it is *the* factor in creating a culture of excellence. This is why the entire middle section of the book is dedicated to trust.

It isn't just a word, or something to flippantly speak about. This is the core of all relationships.

We have things about others we may not like, or that bother us. We also have things that we tolerate in others – meaning we accept, but don't smile about them.

And then, we have things that are deal breakers. You know, the things that break relationships…the end of interaction.

My good friend talks about his relational deal breaker. The one thing that when it happens to him that will bust up everything. Even a decades long relationship can be dismantled in a heartbeat.

You've probably been there or know someone else that has.

This one thing, that when it happens, you find yourself parting ways.

Lying.

Not being truthful or trustworthy is a deal breaker for my friend, and for most people. It is so hard to stay in a relationship, work closely with, or count on someone when you don't trust them.

We tend to hear people say how important trust is for teams. I say it all the time.

Your team culture must be built on trust.

The reality is, your team culture must be built on trust, and the data proves it.

Out of seven potential categories, trust was the number one factor selected when creating a culture of excellence.

Not only did 52% of respondents select it as their number one attribute (see pie chart), over 80% selected trust in their top three!

PERCENTAGE OF WHICH EACH CATEGORY WAS SELECTED AS THE NUMBER ONE ATTRIBUTE

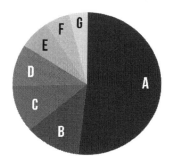

A. The Trust Factor - 51.68%
B. Servant Leadership - 12.08%
C. Working Effectively Together - 10.74%
D. Clear Sight of the Future - 9.39%
E. Everyone is Empowered - 6.71%
F. Extreme Ownership - 5.37%
G. Identify and Adapt to Change - 4.03%

Earlier in the book, I noted that being able to identify and adapt to change was the greatest struggle for teams. 30% of respondents selected it as their team's area of struggle.

Want to guess what number two was?

You are so smart!

The Trust Factor!

So, 80% of people state trust is a top three essential for a team culture, and 16% stated this was their team's number one area of struggle.

Interesting.

We determine from this that not only is trust important, teams are struggling with this as well.

We simply cannot ignore this data.

We simply cannot just say "trust is important."

We must act upon it.

chapter eight

BUILD THE FOUNDATION

When my daughter, Nevaeh, was just a couple years old, one of her favorite things to do was to play a game of catch with me.

Yes, my daughter could play catch at a very young age.

The key: I was the one both tossing and catching.

Her.

That's right, I would stand tall, hold her above my head and toss her in the air as high as I could. She would smile, giggle, and even belly laugh out loud.

The look in her eyes, the expression on her face... priceless. It was so fun to play that way, to enjoy the time together. I miss that toddler stage!

Oh, my, I nearly forgot...yes, I would catch her.

As soon as she would land in my arms she would exclaim with joy, "Again!!!"

We would do this for as long as my old arms could handle it.

We didn't keep a record, yet if I were to guess, I would wager we played catch like this over 500 times.

You know why it worked?

You know why she kept wanting to play?

There's a secret.

Can you guess what it is?

Trust.

I caught her.

Every. Time.

Nevaeh had absolute, complete, and total trust in me. She simply knew I would catch her.

Even though I tossed her hundreds of times, if I dropped her even once, the chances are she would never want to play again.

Trust.

The foundation of it all.

Trust is either being built with every interaction, or it can be completely destroyed in a moment.

Now, think of your team.

Think of the people you work with, live with, share life with.

Do you want to be around people you trust?

Silly question, I know.

Seriously, though, what are you doing to gain trust?

What are you doing to build upon the relational trust you have?

Take a moment and really think about this.

Are you intentionally speaking and behaving in such a manner where trust is being built all the time?

In simple terms, you are either building trust or losing it.

You begin building trust from the first moment you meet someone, and you continue to build it (or lose it) each and every time you interact

You are either building trust or losing it.

with them. Some of the list below may seem obvious, yet we need to remind ourselves of what builds trust.

Here is my top 10 list, in no particular order:

- » Be dependable
- » Speak the truth, always
- » Don't gossip or share confidential information
- » Show a real concern for people
- » Catch people when they are about to fall
- » Pick people back up when they do fall
- » Be helpful to others
- » Give credit and recognition to others
- » Accept responsibility and be accountable
- » Be willing to listen

As you navigate your upcoming interactions with your teams, think about these things. Make a conscious decision to build trust and move your relationship with each of them higher.

As we move forward, you will see why this is so important and how to live it out.

Don't stop now...keep on reading my friends!

chapter nine

STRENGTHEN THE STRUCTURE WITH WHY AND WHAT

Many years ago my wife and I were in the process of a transformation. Our faith journey was deepening, our marriage was as well, and we wanted to ensure our family reached our desired destination.

Not just any destination, our desired one.

We wanted to set a course for our family. We weren't interested in letting the winds of life just take us, our children or future generations just anywhere.

I don't believe you want that for any of your teams either.

We had a purpose in mind and wanted our team, our

family, to know what it was in order to live it out.

I believe you want that too for your teams.

A phrase I use often is, "All roads lead somewhere, just depends on where you want to go."

All roads lead somewhere, just depends on where you want to go.

Your team needs to know where you are going, how to stay aligned on the journey, and have persistence to stay the course.

To do this, your team needs to have complete trust in one another. The materials in your structure of trust are strengthened when everyone knows two key things.

People need to know *why* and *what*.

Why the team is in place and *why* the team exists.

This is the core essence of the organization's purpose.

The understanding of *why* is paramount.

It is about trust.

It is about being transparent, with everyone, as to your purpose, the desired destination and then, the expectations.

The expectations are the *what*.

What is expected, accepted, and not tolerated.

You can call these values, core beliefs, or culture expectations. It doesn't matter what you call them, what matters is that you have them and you share them.

Repeatedly.

Since my family is the most important team in my life, setting the right direction with our *why* and *what* was (and still is) the most important work. The life long and generational impact of us having our desired culture is why my wife and I created our two part value statement for our family.

She then took the words, added a photo from one of our family vacations, framed it, and placed it on a wall in our home.

It is simply called, "Fox Family Values."

Our *why* is derived from two Bible verses. Our *why* is "To love God and love people, and live that out so others will do the same."

Our *what* are the expectations (the behaviors) on how we live this out. These are our 6 core values:

> » Loving
> » Honest
> » Forgiving

47

- » Responsible
- » Hardworking
- » Trustworthy

Your turn.

Does your team have a solid, shared, and focused *why*?

Do you have a vision/mission statement that truly states what your purpose is to exist?

Many organizations have these, if your organization doesn't, now is the time.

Stop reading, set up a meeting and get the right people in the room to hash this out.

You need to have this.

Here are the key questions to ask and answer:

- » Does your purpose revolve around your own needs, or those you serve?
- » Do you have an inward focused vision or an outward one?

To transform your culture into one of excellence, you need to have an outward focused vision. You need to revolve your vision around a destination to serve others.

What do I mean by that?

Your vision is focused on what you provide or do *for* others. This isn't just about providing a service or product, this vision is about making a difference.

You need to do good for the community, your clients, your family and other organizations, and your vision/value statement will reflect this.

Additionally, your list of core values and expectations, those things that are most important, will be the bedrock of your existence.

The team will stand firmly on those principles making it difficult to sway or deviate.

Without those values, without the reinforcement of them, trust is eroded.

There is no morality, ethics, or integrity with a team that doesn't have a shared set of principled beliefs.

Remember, there will be a culture.

Your team will go to a destination.

The question is, which one?

Which culture do you want?

Where do you want to end up?

Too many teams just do work. It is *just* a job. The greater good isn't thought of; it is just about me, myself and I.

In contrast to that, the elite teams have a solid structure, with their *why* focused on others, and a principled value system of *what*. This is where great teams, silver platter service type teams, quickly and dramatically separate themselves from the masses.

Having a purpose greater than yourself, and sticking to it, is not optional, it is essential.

Having a purpose greater than yourself, and sticking to it, is not optional, it is essential.

These teams understand how important it is to develop a sound *why* and *what*. They do so because it is the guiding light for the team to see. It is a core element of gaining trust.

Your work team will thrive if you do this. As you live this out, suppliers, clients, competitors and the community at large will see the difference. And your team will experience the difference.

Your team hungers for this.

They truly do want more than a paycheck.

They want to be in a place they trust and a team that stands for something good. A place that is safe to work and does something together that makes a difference in the world.

This works for your family too. They are starving for this.

Take time today, be intentional, be purposeful, and give them your best. Give them the *why* and *what* for their lives.

chapter ten

SAY SOMETHING, DO SOMETHING

Having written values, mission statements, and culture expectations is important. Now, we will spend the rest of this book focused on living them out.

Saying something is one thing, actually living it out is quite another.

We can all write down words, have meetings talking about what is important, and even promote and publicize how wonderful we are.

Do you hear the sarcasm?

If you individually, and collectively as a team, don't live out what you say, there is zero integrity.

Not some.

Zero.

Trust is about integrity.

It is about doing what you say you will do.

Period.

Always.

You and your team need to live out your words in action that people can see, experience, and know. What you *say* you are isn't *who* you are. You are what you *do*.

> **What you *say* you are isn't *who* you are. You are what you *do*.**

Take this example as a learning opportunity for us.

There is a rather large bank in our country that I will leave nameless due to the nature of this true story. They have core values listed on their website. Here is a quick summary:

> ... every moment matters
> ... our decisions affect people's lives
> ... our decisions are fair and responsible
> ... we do the right thing

So, now that we know who they are and what they stand for, let's see it in action.

A good friend of mine, Mark, shared his experience with me recently with this very large banking enterprise.

Right in the middle of the COVID quarantine, his mom became very ill. The reality, the woman that nurtured him and loved him for his whole life was dying. She was in her early 90's.

She lived a full life, but the passing of anyone, especially Mom, is hard.

Mark was living over 1,000 miles from his mom at the time, and due to the travel lockdowns, he couldn't see his mom even one last time.

This story is not unique.

Unfortunately, neither is the next part.

Upon the passing of his mom, Mark became the executor of her will. In the process of mourning, he had to be the one to deal with the finances, belongings and other legal stuff.

If you've ever had to do it, you know the stress involved.

As he went through the process and paperwork, he came across her credit card bill from the bank. The bank where she had been a client for over 40 years, where he was also a client for over 30 years.

Mark's mom, in the process of her life ending, had missed her last credit card payment due date.

She owed $102 in late fees and interest.

He picked up the phone, called customer service and explained the situation. The agent passed him along to a bereavement department that specializes in handling things of this nature.

Nice, a person that deals with loved ones grieving.

He thought, "Perfect!"

Not so fast, my friends.

The specialist refused his request to waive the fees, not even one cent!

This bank has $150 billion in value, and the agent wouldn't wave $102. So, he moved up to a supervisor.

Who also refused to waive the fees.

In a final attempt, Mark asked the employee, would your CEO (and he named the CEO) be able to waive this?

The agent said, "No he wouldn't."

There you have it.

So much for "every moment matters," "decisions are fair and responsible," or "we do the right thing."

There is zero empowerment here. Zero real care for the customer.

There is only policy, policy, policy.

There is no human relationship building or excellence in service. This is standing ground on policy, as a result of poor culture.

Poor leadership, poor training, poor everything.

Remember this:

You need to ensure your purpose for people is always greater than your policy for profit!

Now, profit isn't just a monetary thing for a profit-based business. Any team can profit from their policies.

Schools care about test scores, non-profit organizations about donations, and yes, businesses about cash profits.

You need to ensure your purpose for people is always greater than your policy for profit!

Having goals and paying attention to those details matters. Yet, your values and living them out matters more.

This bank has written values. The words say they care. Their actions speak otherwise. Living out your values is hard, but it is the part of building trust that matters more than anything else.

People inside and outside of your team need to know

that when you say something, you do something, you follow through.

You need to live out your values, each and every moment.

Like this.

Marriott International is in the business of serving people, travelers to be exact. From families on vacation, to the road warrior professionals like me, they aim to be excellent in serving them all.

Their core values, from their website, include several really great statements:

> ... values are who we are
> ... beliefs are most important
> ... beliefs stay the same
> ... putting people first
> ... pursuing excellence
> ... embracing change
> ... acting with integrity
> ... serving our world

Cool. Sounds like they have read parts of this book!

I'm very loyal as a traveler to their brand, and here is one example why.

After an event in Indianapolis, I checked out of the Fairfield Inn, tossed my things into the trunk of the Uber driver's car, and off to the airport we went. I had time to get through security and walk to my gate, with a little bit of time to spare.

As I approached the TSA checkpoint, I reached into my backpack and realized I had left a bag in my hotel room. This bag was essential, as it contained medication that I'm prescribed to take daily.

Due to my lack of planning, I didn't allow for anything to go wrong.

Well, it had.

I was either going to miss the plane to get my bag, or I would make my flight and would not have the bag. Decision made, I had to be on the flight to make my next engagement.

Frantically, I called the hotel.

I explained my situation, provided my name and room number, and asked if they could find the belongings and ship them to my next hotel.

What felt like five hours later was actually five minutes later when my phone rang. I picked it up and heard a familiar voice.

"I have your bag Mr. Fox. No worries, I'm in my car and I'll be at the airport in less than 15 minutes. Will that be enough time for you to meet me outside and still make your flight?"

My new best friend from Marriott was driving my bag to the airport in his own car!

Turned out he was the assistant manager of the hotel and he was living out the values of his organization.

Did it cost money and time for him to do this?

Sure it did.

Were there other things he was supposed to be doing?

Probably.

Was it policy to get in your personal car on business time to help a client?

I don't know, but he did it.

That happened years ago, and I can still see his face as he met me outside the airport. His smile was as big as mine. Oh, yeah, and I made my flight *with* my bag.

See, you need to do what you say you will do.

You build trust when you show that people matter more. That is excellence in service and that is how you create a culture of excellence.

As you keep on reading, you will find a variety of great examples on how to bring people together, serve others, and change cultures to deliver silver platter service.

chapter eleven

TRIUMPH WITH TRANSPARENCY

In 2008, our country went through what is now referred to as the Financial Crisis. This great recession was massive, hard-hitting, with ripple effects that lasted for nearly a decade.

I was employed as the Director of Marketing at Jet, a privately held plastic card manufacturing company of about $35 million, with 200 employees. The printing industry was no different than any other, and even though we were a profitable and growing company, our business declined.

Jeff Norby was the President, and Tony Haugen was our Senior Vice President, and my friend for many years. As the top executives, they led the "council of 12" leaders heading up the direction of the company. I was honored to be at that table.

We knew as a group, with Jeff and Tony at the helm, how we communicated and handled things was paramount. Protecting the company wasn't just a financial position and strategy, protecting the company meant protecting the people.

Sometimes tough decisions need to be made.

This is where we realize, not all change is good when it is happening. It isn't always rainbows and unicorns in the constant pursuit of an excellent culture.

To ensure we served our clients well, and continued to be excellent for years to come, we had to make some tough decisions.

In short, we had to let people go.

No fault of their own.

We just didn't have enough business to support our payroll.

15% of our team was being let go.

This had never happened at Jet, ever. In over 60 years, no one had been laid off.

Additionally, everyone staying would receive a

pay cut of 5%. These two moves together would buy us time to recover.

Jeff worked with us to put together plans on how we would roll this out. One key element he insisted on was transparency throughout the grueling process.

One key method we used for this was what we termed as "Employee Town Hall Meetings."

These meetings were held the first Friday of every month, for months on end. The entire company was invited. We actually held multiple meetings on those Fridays since we had multiple shifts and two facilities.

In advance of the meeting, Jeff would ask the 12 of us for agenda items we wanted him to address. It was his way of ensuring that those of us leading the teams presented him with concerns employees had, so he could speak to specific issues.

At every meeting, as Jeff concluded his remarks, he did two really important things.

First, he provided the opportunity for any of the 12 of us leaders to speak on any topic. Any topic, and without rehearsal or clearing our remarks prior to the meeting.

Secondly, he opened the floor for the entire company to ask questions. The meeting didn't end until every employee that wanted to raise their hand had the opportunity to do so.

Jeff would answer every one of them, every time.

Now, I understand that you may not be in a crisis right now. Or maybe you are.

Either way, don't miss out on this key moment.

This wasn't about politicking or marketing or spinning visions to underlings. This wasn't just some fluffy announcement telling the staff things they wanted to hear.

He was totally transparent.

Real facts. Real truth.

Good or bad, the truth was spoken.

This is what it means to change culture.

This is how you become excellent.

No matter how big or small your team may be, if you aren't using transparent, open, two-way dialogue as part of your consistent methodology, you aren't pursuing excellence.

This might seem harsh or blunt, but this is the truth.

How can a team create a culture of excellence without a culture of trust?

How do you create trust if you aren't willing to speak openly?

How can a team believe in the changes ahead if no one is clearly defining, describing and casting the vision?

How do you expect loyalty, employee engagement,

and great results if people aren't respected enough to simply share the truth?

The answer to those four questions is the same.

You can't.

The trust factor can never be about anything other than complete honesty.

Trust mandates that we not hide or give partial information.

Trust demands that we share, openly and honestly.

Building trust is never about building up the leader; it is about building up the team.

The leader is followed when people believe the leader has intentions for their best interest.

The culture improves because trust grows.

No matter how hard the circumstances, with transparency, trust grows.

Building trust is never about building up the leader; it is about building up the team.

With heartfelt empathy and good communication, people listen.

With actions that back up the words, people believe.

With consistency in these things, your culture can become excellent.

Jeff didn't always have great answers for some of the employees' questions. Heck, sometimes he didn't have any answer.

In those cases, he would look at his 12 leaders, and one of us would say, "I'll take that one."

From there, we would either answer at that time, or say, "We will discuss and look into it and have an answer for you next week."

Saying "I don't know and I'll get back to you" is actually far better than trying to show you know everything.

Trust isn't gained by having all the answers, it is about leading people in the pursuit of the answers.

> **Trust isn't gained by having all the answers, it is about leading people in the pursuit of the answers.**

The team that shares openly, welcomes questions, and pursues the best solutions together, will win.

In our case, we eventually did win.

Like how those amazing structural buildings took time to be constructed, so did our journey.

About six months into our town halls, the entire company understood that our culture would be one of trust. It was based on open communication and the importance of each person.

Our business slowly began to rebound.

And then it happened.

One town hall meeting, Jeff surprised us all.

He announced that the 5% pay cuts were being restored.

Everyone would be back to the pay level from six months ago!

And then he added that all of the pay that had been subtracted was retroactively being returned in the next paycheck.

Talk about building trust.

It was an amazing day.

It was an even more amazing gesture to say that people mattered. But wait, there's more...steak knives (just kidding!).

Jeff did have one more item he announced that infamous day. The four top executives that had reduced their pay were not restoring their wages to the previous levels.

They were leading first.

They communicated that transparency was

paramount, and trust in the team was a cultural must.

That low time in our company, from our plummeting revenues, our lowering profits and down spirits were quickly replaced with the largest growth in our company's history.

It had taken nearly 60 years to reach 35 million dollars in annual revenue. In just five short years after the worst economic downturn since the Great Depression, we doubled.

That's right. We hit 70 million dollars of revenue in just five years.

True story.

I lived through it.

I was fortunate to participate with a front row seat on an amazing journey. Our team culture was built on integrity, trust, open communication, and a commitment to serving our clients.

We won because transparency took first place and was cemented in who we were as a team.

We won because people trusted the leadership.

We won because even when things were down, the team knew Jeff (and all of us really) had their best interest at hand.

The employees and the clients were more important than the bottom line.

Pretty cool how our focus on people helped the company achieve record-setting top and bottom line numbers.

You know what is even more cool?

You can too.

Trust me!

chapter twelve

SOME THINGS SHOULD NEVER CHANGE

As we look at industries around our country, the big players seem to just gobble up or take out the little guy.

Big box retailers are gone, like Woolworths, Borders, even places like shopping malls are being eliminated as our buying culture changes. Amazon, apps and other online purchases, have radically changed the landscape. So has the amount of marketing dollars the big companies like Capital One, Bank of America and others spend on TV advertising? They simply outpace the smaller organizations.

Or do they?

One of the clients I have been honored to deliver keynotes for is a great team. In fact, I first became aware of them because it is where I used to bank when I lived in Illinois.

Libertyville Bank and Trust is a Wintrust Community Bank, located in the suburbs of Chicago. And, with so many large banking brands, competition is fierce.

Rachel Vincent is the Executive Vice President of retail banking, and as you can imagine from her title, her job is to grow the business. She was the 21st employee at Libertyville Bank & Trust in what is now over 120 in their group, and over 5,000 employees in the entire Wintrust network of community banks.

Regardless of what field you work in, the size of your organization, the town you live in, how much money you have or don't, or your educational background, there is much for us to learn from Rachel and her team.

Some of the founding members of the bank are still with the company. They came from big banks and were frustrated. They created this bank to build better relationships. They believed too many organizations and corporations were making distant decisions, away from, and not in touch with, the customer.

And so, Libertyville Bank and Trust was formed. Now some 25 years later, business is still growing.

Why?

Because of what they focus on. Because of what *doesn't* change.

I know what you are thinking. You are thinking this whole book started with change and how change agents must be our fuel to the future.

Yes, that is true.

However, (there is always a however, right?), you must change for progress, not change your purpose.

Some things shouldn't change.

Ever.

Like your *why*.

Libertyville Bank and Trust was founded on relationships and their *why* is to serve well.

That cannot and doesn't change.

Just look at their name, trust is in it. Now, I understand that is a legal term, yet how do you have trust in your name and not build it, right? Trust is so critical, and they know (and so should you) that they need to have real relationships with their customers in order to establish and build trust.

Trust begins with who you bring on board.

You must change for progress, not change your purpose.

Rachel shared how they have to be very careful with hiring. It is way more than finding talent, a great resume or vast industry experience.

It is about mindset and behavior.

The mindset needs to be one of community focus.

Being qualified isn't enough, you have to be aligned with their vision of serving the community. They don't want coin operated employees, who just check boxes or work some rubric.

They need, and hire, people-focused people.

Furthermore, every role matters. The behavior needs to be one of ownership, that every part and every person contributes to the organization, the community and the customer.

In short, they look for people who love people and are filled with character.

Check out what Rachel shared with me: "Our business is driven on behaviors, not numbers and results. We offer relationships, not sales. And this evolves over time. We don't have quotas on our bankers.

We focus on ethics, on their *why*, on customers, on ownership. Our approach is to take absolute great care of our customer, and the results will happen. Each employee is unique, each customer is unique, so we look to create alignment with our customers' needs and help match them.

We realize that what may be best for a customer may not be with us."

Check that out.

They are willing to let customers walk out the door. If what is in the best interest of the customer is found somewhere else, then they help them land there.

Wow.

And did you catch the earth shattering statement she made early on?

They don't have quotas.

None.

Zero.

How about that for standing in the face of sales management 101.

I worked for over 20 years for companies large and small. We always had quotas. There were quotas for sales, quotas for operations, quotas for safety, quotas for quality and on and on and on.

The problem with quotas is that the sale can become more important than the customer.

Now, it doesn't mean Rachel and her team don't have business goals. It doesn't mean they don't forecast, or set plans in place and expect growth.

They do all of that.

And they are doing it well.

The point is, they don't place a quota on a person and drive behavior based on sales.

They drive outcomes based on behavior focused on serving people and the needs of the customer.

Don't miss this.

Because the customer knows the banker works for the best interest of the customer, trust is built.

That trust becomes a loyal business customer, who then, in turn, tells their friends. It now becomes a cycle of the best marketing ever known in the history of the world, word of mouth.

Keep that in mind as we head back to our main idea in this chapter of what should and shouldn't change.

How we communicate is changing, rapidly. The bankers used to just sit with clients, now they might FaceTime or interface through other technologies, online services, and apps.

The methods may change, technology changes, *how* you do things will change.

But, the value and personal touch is what doesn't change.

You don't change why you do things.

Keep it personal.

Rachel and her team still handwrite thank you cards.

They call people personally on the phone.

Yes, it's more *efficient* to mass email.

However, it is more *effective* to keep things personal.

They built a culture on a *why*. To this day, they keep their main *why* the same.

During COVID-19, Wintrust Community Banks processed and funded over 10,000 Paycheck Protection Program small business loans in just the first round. For a community bank group, that is amazing.

This was because everyone on their team jumped in. People in other departments were helping to process loans. People worked 16-hour days to make this happen.

The team stepped up to do the right thing because they knew it was the right thing to do. It was their way of living out their *why*.

All for one reason.

They knew they were helping people in a great time of need.

It wasn't an anomaly, this is their culture. It was intentional, repeated and effective.

And, as Rachel humbly shared, "We were proud to serve."

That, my friends, is what never changes.

You and your team must be proud to serve.

Not proud to sell.

Not just focused on the next quota or next marketing strategy.

Proud to help, to make a difference, to serve and be there for your clients.

There is a reason this small business is booming. They are different from the other big banks.

People know they care about them and because of that, they trust them.

Sure, everyone knows they are a for-profit business, but I can tell you from firsthand experience as a client, I never felt like a piece of business. I mattered, my family mattered, and what was important to me was important to them.

The main question for you is this: How consistent, and successful, are you at building trust and growing relationships through acts of service to others?

Focus on that and never let it change!

chapter thirteen

PEOPLE MATTER MOST

Sometimes in life we simply come across an organization that embodies what it means to care for people. They show us that people matter most.

In an earlier chapter I said, "People matter more." I was incorrect.

People matter *most*!

This was certainly the case when I was introduced to Union University in Jackson, Tennessee, where our eldest son, Trevor, went to college.

I can still remember that beautiful fall day when the two of us drove onto campus together. This was our first stop of several, over a couple of months, visiting five different universities.

One thing that we found in common at each campus visit, each one had a unique culture.

One of the universities continued to stress how important their academic excellence was, they believed they were the best in the world (I humbly disagree). Another university focused on how proud they were of all their new beautiful buildings which cost hundreds of millions of dollars (that was an interesting cultural focal point).

One of our visits was at a very small school that asked us to sign a covenant behavior contract at the end of the tour (that was more than interesting).

In fairness, all five schools are truly great schools. In the end, the visits were about helping us see who they were beyond statistics and websites. We wanted to better understand their culture, and we did.

Union University was completely different. They were all about relationships.

As you can see in the picture, they had a parking spot with Trevor's name on it ready for us.

Funny thing, I was so nervous pulling into the lot I just grabbed the first spot I saw and stopped, so we didn't see it until after our tour was over. I moved our car over later so we could take the photo, ha!

On the tour, our guide made numerous mentions of how much he liked Dub.

I kept wondering who or what Dub was?

Finally, I had to ask. I learned Dub is short for Dr. Samuel W. "Dub" Oliver, the President of Union University, or UU as we call it. It was apparent Dub was not your typical University President.

The student guiding us around couldn't stop talking about how much they loved Dub, and how he would call students by name as he walked around campus. They made such a big deal about how he treated them. How he attended events, invited students to lunch with him, and the list went on and on.

And unlike our other stops, every staff member we met seemed to be like this infamous Dub. They truly cared about us, spending time getting to know us and how they could help Trevor in this season of his life.

Most campuses wanted to sell us on them, while UU wanted to simply help find Trevor's next best. As our time concluded at UU that day, we knew it was someplace special.

A couple weeks later we set up a Skype call with Professor Beverly, the head of the broadcasting department. I'll skip through the formalities to the end of our call.

I can still see his face and hear his great voice (he broadcasted sports for decades) as he said, "Trevor, if you choose to come here to UU, I promise we will do our best to give you an education, maybe not the best one, but a good one. More importantly, I promise you for certain, we will love you."

Wow!!!

My mom and dad worked in education for over 20 years, so I grew up around educators. I went to college and I have numerous friends who are great teachers.

Yet, until that moment, I had never heard an educator make a "we will love you" promise. A promise about the person and their relationship.

This was a promise to care for our son.

This was a statement about their culture.

People mattered most.

And you know what? This wasn't just talk, they lived it out.

Trevor has shared so many stories about how relationships were built from day one, and how UU leaders invested in him.

From the start, the UU staff placed each student in a Life Group. These groups exist to build relationships. They help students during their first year connect with other students, meet friends, navigate life on campus and be cared for by older students. Trevor actually became one of these mentoring leaders while on campus.

Another example of their relationship building is through what they call "Be Our Guest." Students go online and sign up to go to dinner at the house of a professor or administrator. The spots are limited per night and location, yet they could choose any open spot they wished.

What a great way to get to know people, share food and get beyond academics.

All of these intentional and lived out moments remind us of this important truth when it comes to building trust:

Building trust comes down to authentic relationships. It's all about relationships.

We visited the UU campus a couple of times while our son was in school, and the same feelings from my first visit were still there. What an amazing group of people loving on young adults as they prepare for their next season in life.

We met faculty that spoke about students as if they were their own children. The pride and dreams they had for each of them. They were invested in the

Building trust comes down to authentic relationships. It's all about relationships.

students, the person, not just the grades or the money or their own faculty status.

Graduation time came and what a wonderful celebration of hard work done, the life ahead and yes, the emotions too. It became a bit more emotional as I watched Trevor walk across the stage and receive not a handshake, but a big bear hug from Dub just after he received his diploma.

Again, wow!

Unlike many schools, he didn't receive a diploma cover that contained nothing inside (we'll mail you your diploma later).

Nor like many other colleges, this wasn't a mass print of the diploma where the only thing personalized was his name.

I understand why universities do this. Hey, it does the job, it's legal, and it's efficient.

There is nothing wrong with that. It gets the job done.

But, it's not Silver Platter Service.

Or cultural excellence.

That isn't UU, nor is it Dub.

A few weeks prior to graduation, Dub begins his personal touch of yet another relational moment for each graduate. Dub sits at his desk, prays over each graduate's name and personally signs over 550 diplomas.

Amidst COVID-19, graduation at UU, like so many other campuses, became an online event. Dub still found a way to be very personal.

He recorded the personal and individual signing of

each diploma, with a message to each graduate. 565 personal videos were created by him and sent to each family. This took him over 50 hours, yet that is what makes their culture so great.

My friends, this type of culture where people matter most doesn't just happen.

This isn't just a mission statement or words on the wall.

This isn't a marketing catch phrase to get more business.

This isn't fake and done for a moment or two.

While it is true, people-focused is part of the UU mission statement, it is more than words. They are all intentional about living it out.

For example, in contrast to most universities, even smaller ones, they keep their faculty to student ratio at an amazingly low 1:10. In reference to personal bonding, over 80% of students have been a guest in a faculty member's home.

This is a lifestyle.

People matter most.

This is UU.

This is cultural excellence.

This is how everyone that works at UU lives their

daily lives. This is not exceptional at UU, this is natural, expected and simply the way they live and work.

In short, they go out of the way to love people, all people.

They want the best for each student and for one another. They want to help when they can, support when needed, laugh and cry when appropriate, and celebrate the victories.

Speaking of celebrations, we had a graduation party at our home in Florida in May of 2019.

Two of Trevor's professors (a married couple) were very special to him while he was on campus.

He confided in them for professional and personal advice. Out of respect and thanks, Trevor invited them to our party.

Remember, they all live in Tennessee, we are in Florida.

It just so happened, though, they were vacationing as a family that same week in Florida. Spoiler alert... what I'm about to share shouldn't surprise you.

They adjusted their driving route (meaning they went out of their way) to include a stop at our home to celebrate Trevor, meet us and wish him well. I literally had a hard time saying goodbye to them. I was so touched. Thank you, Blairs, for loving our son.

From our first visit to our final celebration, UU is special because the people are special.

Dub is their leader, yet he would never be so bold to claim anything more than he is blessed to work with them all. He, and the staff at UU, embody what it means to live out the phrase, "People Matter Most."

The question for you and your team is, how well do you live this out?

Does your team naturally and consistently put people first?

Are people just a means to the end (the bottom line) or are people the bottom line?

Do people truly matter most? Do your actions, individually and collectively, focus on people or on something else?

Here's a tough one for you:

Are people just a means to the end (the bottom line) or are people the bottom line?

If you truly want employee engagement, employee empowerment and client satisfaction, put people first.

If you want to gain trust from others, you need to show you care about them.

Always.

Why?

In order for people to trust you, they need to know one thing for certain:

People matter most!

BRINGING EVERYONE TOGETHER

section three

chapter fourteen

WE'RE ENGAGED!

Marriage is a big deal.

Marriage is about loving and sharing life with someone for the rest of your life. It's an important decision. It's a gift from God – a blessing – and should be marked by special moments. Prior to the wedding ceremony, the first special moment is the proposal.

The proposal begins the commitment, the expression of love and the promise. The proposal is important.

I remember the planning that was involved prior to popping the question to my now wife, Marne. There were hours of thought involved. Details to work out for our dinner, a poem to write/frame, flowers to order, how to ask, and when/how to reveal the ring.

In short, there was a plan.

Great news, she said "Yes!"

From that moment, came the engagement. The beginning of a commitment to one another that leads  to the wedding, and ultimately, a life of marriage. Together.

We're finding that even after our wedding ceremony, remaining "engaged" in our marriage is more important. There are important steps to remain engaged with one another. The effort to "date" each other, to listen to one another, to spend time together, and to work at life together is a must.

As we say in our home, "We have to be on the same page."

The constant communication between us and our ability to collaborate is key to effectively living together.

And the same is true for your team.

How engaged is your team?

How intentional are you in ensuring that they are focused on your mission, vision, and values in all they do?

Our research showed that behind trust, the second most important element in creating a culture of excellence is a team working effectively *together*.

The reality is, in order to work effectively together, your team must be fully engaged.

They need to be empowered and released to make a difference.

Let's see this in action.

Beginning in 2018, the Kalamazoo Southeast Employees Credit Union (KALSEE), set out to transform a transaction culture to a relationship-building culture.

There was just one problem. They really didn't know exactly how to accomplish this transformation.

With a motto of "Our family, serving yours," April Ridgeway, Organizational Development Manager, knew that motto was the place to begin.

She, and the leadership team, looked at ways in which they would live out the aspect of being a family. How would they serve one another and their members as family?

Saying it is one thing, doing it is quite another.

After many discussions and strategy sessions, April knew there needed to be actionable changes. It began with their new hires. On the first day of their training session she says to them, "If you aren't passionate about serving people, this isn't the place for you."

That statement meant they had to be willing to watch people walk away. Whether they stay or go, their focus is on what is actually best for both parties.

Next, the leadership team wanted team members to connect with *why* they come to work everyday, and to define what truly makes KALSEE different from their competitors.

They set out to establish their *why* by participating in a collaborative workshop with more than a third of their team. April explained the process:

"We shared stories on what made us feel proud to work at KALSEE. In those stories, we identified our contribution and what impact we made as a result. The process gave us our new mission statement: *We believe in building relationships and cultivating financial wellness, empowering people to focus on what matters.* We also received something else. We have seen a deeper connection with our team members owning the value they bring to our members."

What a great example of engaging a team. One leader didn't just tell the team the *why* and *what*, instead, they built it together.

And they just kept bringing everyone together as they turned the focus on relationship-building as a core training element.

The KALSEE leadership implemented an 8-week service program called The Member Advantage ®. Every single team member goes through the program: new hire or 30-year veteran.

Everyone.

This program teaches the team members skills in effective communication to build relationships. Elements include how to have good conversations, communicating with different types of people, how to ask good questions, and how to provide value to others based on their members' needs.

Notice how the focus is on others, on serving them, not on selling them.

To really make the most impact, they needed to focus on the face of the organization. The people who have the most interaction with the members.

The teller.

Most of us are familiar with this title. The person that stands behind the counter and processes your transaction.

Remember, April's team was trying to move from transaction-based to relationship-building.

The problem with "teller" as a title is they noticed it created a mindset. They would hear, "I can't do that, I'm just a teller."

Just. Hmmm.

The person that interfaces with the client the most thinks they are "just" something, and therefore are not empowered.

Teller sounds like, and is, a transaction processor.

They needed to change this "just" attitude to continue to change the culture.

They redefined the role and re-titled it to Member Experience Representative (MER). April shared, "We wanted them to have conversations. We needed to empower them and make our expectations clear. Relationship-building isn't an add-on, it is at the core of what you do and who you are."

A new title is one thing, now for a full redefinement. Time for full engagement.

They created tiered roles. As the team member gains experience, they receive ongoing training and development. Bottom line, there are opportunities to advance. There are three levels, and each comes with a change in title, pay, and added responsibilities, including leading the less experienced MERs.

This empowered the front line team members to have pride and to own the membership experience. It encouraged self-driven growth, engagement at KALSEE, and increased member experience.

And it worked.

April and her team started measuring employee engagement during this period of transformation. With the national average for employee engagement around 33%, in 2018, KALSEE was just below that at 31%. With these intentional changes, just about a year later, employee engagement rose to 52%!

Then, they started seeing metrics rise too.

The MER at their largest branch completed the Member Advantage Program and was part of the new tiered program. In just her first year she won the top MER for cross sales.

Not only that, her number was a new record of 330, eclipsing the old record by doubling it!

She attests her success to the implementation of the skills learned, the empowerment provided, and the impact it makes to the team.

Do you think having a career path for your team which unleashes their relationship power matters?

You bet it does!

Do you want to know what's even more impressive? April and the KALSEE team thought it might take years to surpass that new 330 record-setting new standard.

Nope.

It took ONE.

One quarter that is. In just the first quarter of 2020, a MER hit 368 in cross sales. A new annual record set in just one quarter!

The entire team is chasing after that record now.

They have completely shifted their results because

they completely shifted their culture.

This has shifted hiring as well. They now hire people for who they are, not only the experience they have.

Let's all learn from that, and remember this:

Hire for who people are, not only for what they've done!
_____

Hire for who people are, not only for what they've done!

As I previously shared, change takes time. And it was no different here at KALSEE. April shared that it has taken a solid 18 months to apply these principles. Yet totally worth the journey.

Friends, working effectively together to change results starts by engaging your team.

With a proposal.

The question is, "Will you do this with me?"

When your team says "*Yes!*," your culture will change.

Based on this, here are three questions for you to consider:

> » Where in your organization can you make these types of adjustments?

» How can you empower people to build relationships?

» What will you do to make meaningful change in your employee development so you make monumental changes in your results?

chapter fifteen

YOU CREATE WHAT YOU CELEBRATE

For more than 25 years I've been associated with the NCAA as a women's basketball official. It is a great honor, and challenging responsibility to be a referee.

With that said, I have another question for you.

Would you like to be a referee?

Are you willing to get in front of people that are biased to one team, ignorant of the rules, and simply don't like people in black and white stripes?

For nearly all of you, I know the answer:
"No thanks."

You know how I knew your response? We have a massive shortage of officials.

I believe one of the main reasons for that shortage is because we don't celebrate officials.

(Please hang in here with me, this isn't a pity party for refs, I'm actually going somewhere.)

No one likes refs. People don't like it when someone else has control over them.

Fans, coaches, and players all want control of the calls. Even the media wants control, or at least to question the calls.

Yet, no one is stepping up to actually *make the calls.*

Here's the main point.

Being a referee is a rather thankless position. The best officials are those that walk in the back door, do an amazingly fabulous job, leave out the back door, and no one remembers they were even there.

It is rare that anyone thanks officials.

We have, unfortunately, seen fans storming fields and courts to assault officials over what they deemed as a missed call. Maybe it was missed, who knows. That behavior, though, is deplorable.

Unfortunately, there is another less noticeable problem that drives people out of officiating.

It causes the team to break down, it lowers morale, and hurts performance.

This not-so-obvious dilemma has been caused by people like me, the Coordinator of Officials.

The trend has been for the "bosses" to only reach out to officials when they receive video plays of missed calls. Coordinators reach out when officials kick a rule, or mishandle communication, or disrespect someone.

Officials tend to hear from us when they make mistakes. Everyone shows the replay video of mistakes on jumbo screens. The majority of the time, feedback is given on mistakes.

No wonder we have a shortage.

What doesn't happen often enough is communication when they do something good. Not enough high fives for a job well done. Too few thank you's for their effort and impact for the cause. A shortage of simple acts or words of affirmation to say, "I get you, I'm with you, we are in this together."

Last year, I was at one of the Conference Championship games and noticed something in the pre-game warm ups. As one team was running through their drills, every time a player passed by a teammate, they slapped hands.

There was a constant reminder that they were in this together. They were a team, a unit.

I've also experienced this from team members in the officiating community.

It was a warm August day in 2011. My family was at a minor league baseball game, in part, to watch our son play the national anthem with his school band. A good day.

Then it became a great day.

My phone rang, it was my good friend, and fellow official, Jeff Cross.

"Congratulations, Randy!" Jeff had so much enthusiasm in his voice.

"For what?" I replied.

He said, "You made it, you are a Division 1 referee!"

Now, he wasn't my boss, yet he certainly made me feel special in that moment. He knew that becoming a Division 1 referee had been a goal of mine for many years.

He also knew the announcements of new hires were happening that day, and if someone was added to the staff they would appear on the online roster. Jeff saw me on the roster and gave me a call.

Not just to me either. Jeff made a call to every new hire, year after year. He took time to celebrate people and the milestones in their lives.

Jeff has stepped up his celebration game even further over the last few years. Now, if he works with someone on their first Division 1 game, he brings them a gift. Something to commemorate the moment.

Maybe an engraved plaque, or some swag from the conference.

People feel good, people smile, and you know what else, they immediately know they are an important part of the team. They feel like they belong. Jeff takes time to celebrate his teammates.

People love Jeff. They trust him.

The result?

A stronger team.

In turn, they work hard. They believe in themselves. The teamwork improves and overall performance does as well.

I have had the honor of working on the court with Jeff many times in my career. I felt very comfortable working with him as a teammate. You know what I felt even more than comfort?

A responsibility to be my best. To work hard. To show I deserved the celebrations I had received. To return the favor and celebrate others too.

Working effectively together in this manner moves you from co-workers to a family. You truly do life together.

For this to solidify, you need to be intentional about spending time together, outside of work. Building relationships matters.

Celebrations matter.

If you want a culture based on fear, then only notice people when they do something wrong.

If you want a culture where no one takes risks, attack every new idea as impractical.

If you want a culture that is "me" based, don't ask people about their lives or celebrate their success, just celebrate your own.

Let's stop here, you don't want any of that.

You create what you celebrate.

To create a culture that trusts, that tries, that takes risks, that cares about the team, that truly wants excellence, you need to pay very close attention to what you celebrate. Why?

You create what you celebrate.

People respond to positive reinforcement. People will continue to do more of, and even a better job with, the things you celebrate. They also bond together in ways you wouldn't imagine.

Take time to celebrate your team. If you need some help, here are a few ideas:

» Surprise someone with a handwritten note
» Call someone just to say you appreciate them
» Have a social (ice cream, pizza, drinks, soda,

donuts, coffee, whatever) and don't tie it to results, just have a team social

» Catch people doing something right, and praise them loudly, publicly
» When someone fails trying something new to help the team, thank them for being bold and courageous
» Thank your suppliers and partners for being a part of your success; buy them lunch for a change
» Find creative ways to systematically celebrate good work and the behaviors you desire (I will illustrate a great example in the next chapter)

As we wrap up celebrations, it's important to acknowledge that people are going to make mistakes. This doesn't mean we accept poor performance. Rather, we focus on the behaviors desired and we reinforce them. We celebrate catching people doing something good.

Start celebrating the things you want more of in your culture, because what you celebrate is what you create.

You know what happens when your team has this type of genuine "I appreciate you" behavior?

It changes your culture.

chapter sixteen

WE ARE FAMILY

It is my pleasure to introduce you to Tim Widiker, Superintendent at St. Croix Central School District in Wisconsin. He, and the entire district team, are on a quest to be the absolute best they can be.

They do focus on academics, yet even more so on their culture and character.

Their journey requires a culture change and solidification of that transformation. I'm happy to report, they are making great progress.

Tim shared, "Our progress is grounded in a guiding principle: *Kids deserve it.*"

They make every decision based on this principle, which means, at times, the work is harder for staff. But, *kids deserve it.*

Tim is aware that staff is sometimes disappointed

with certain decisions, including how the district hires. Yet, if the guiding principle is followed, the right call is made. Why?

Kids deserve it.

Tim continued to add, "We've hired over 150 people in the last seven years, and I know this for sure:

Experience is overrated. We need people that love kids. This is about kids and about not messing with our culture. We need people to be aligned. Training and development we can teach, yet the alignment piece must be present from day one."

What I have seen from their team, employee engagement is key to their success and hitting their goals. This engagement, when done correctly, helps kids. Remember, *kids deserve it.*

In order to create this environment, though, staff attendance is important. He needs people, their best asset, their best resources to show up.

So does your team.

Many organizations – and schools are no different – struggle with consistent attendance. It is a very sticky subject, so let me be clear here.

No one should be going to work sick or if there is an emergency in their life. The pandemic has reminded us: If you are sick, stay home.

The point is, Tim wanted to do what most teams need

to do, which is eliminate the discretionary absences so that the best products and services are provided each day.

Why? *The kids deserve it.* Your customer deserves it. *Your team deserves it.*

I promised you a great example of how engagement, empowerment, celebrating, purpose, culture and excellence all come together. Here it is.

This is not a top down approach, rather a movement right from the team members themselves.

Several district team members came up with a great idea to address the increasing number of absences among staff. Instead of focusing on consequences and the poor behavior, they reinforced the desired one.

About five years ago the idea became a reality, and the attendance celebration program was launched. It is called, "Monthly Perfect Attendance Drawing."

Each and every staff member that has perfect attendance for that month is placed into the drawing. Their district has three main buildings, so they conduct a drawing for each area, for a total of three drawings.

Each member is celebrated in recognition for their achievement, and the random winners each receive a $50 gift card.

The team loves it!

Not only do they appreciate the added monetary bonus, the recognition from the celebration is even more valuable.

You may be asking, "Randy, doesn't this cost extra money?"

Yes, yes it does.

So they got creative. They use the rewards from their credit card, so it costs nothing from the budget. It is a free reward used to celebrate those helping keep the team at their best.

They even added a year-end perfect attendance award and recognition. Just another way to say thank you and honor their family.

Celebrating creates engagement. Engaged team members take ownership and are empowered. Being intentional and systematic with decisions and processes, Tim and the team are well on their way to bringing everyone together. And by doing likewise, your team will be too.

Tim shared this about being intentional and systematic: "A key element for us is how I can communicate. We are family, I say it all the time, yet I have to live it. Every email and video I send to our entire staff is entitled "Panther family." We are not coworkers, this is truly my family. We do well together as a family."

Even what they wear is systematic, and intentional. They dress a certain way on certain days. On professional development days, they don't wear jeans and t-shirts. They send a message that they are professional educators and take their own learning seriously.

As we have said before, and will share once again, *a culture of excellence is about living out values.* Tim reinforces the premise that their role is to prepare students, serve their community, and help prepare future generations.

During COVID-19, Tim's district made the decision (rightly so and without hesitation) to continue to provide food for all students in need. And this wasn't just in Wisconsin, we saw this around the nation. Many districts opened up schools, made lunches and then had drive up lines to allow parents/guardians to come pickup meals.

St. Croix Central took a different approach.

The team used an online portal to receive orders, and/or other specifics for each family. Food team members came in each morning and prepared the meals. Once complete, meals were ready to be served.

Instead of setting up a car line, though, they decided to set up a volunteer team. The sign up sheet went out, with an invitation for staff members to donate their time to deliver the meals. Who was the first person to sign up? Tim, of course!

Leaders lead first.

And they served their Panther family, literally.

Within a few hours, the sign up sheet was filled through the end of the school year. The volunteers came to school each day, loaded the meals onto the school bus, and delivered them.

With a transportation team member at the wheel, the volunteer staff member would navigate them to each and every home for the entire district. That's right, they personally delivered the meals directly to each family's home. Check out the smiles in that photo!

To clarify this silver platter service, no team members were asking for a new contract or a raise. No one asked for compensation or time off. It was simply their pleasure to serve their family.

What an impact this has made.

Through the work of engagement and celebration, this team took that personal level of celebration and appreciation to every home.

The opportunity to serve, to connect, to extend real community to the Panther family will never be forgotten.

Again, these are intentional, now systematic parts of their culture. Why did they do it?

Kids deserve it!

Do they want higher test scores?

Sure.

Do they want to be a top school?

You bet.

And they are.

Four years ago, St. Croix School District started at 134th out of 368 K–12 districts. They are now 71st. That is great progress.

Again, this example isn't really about testing and academics. This example shows what happens when you focus on culture and character transformation. Tim and the team focus on that, not on the outcomes.

To obtain your culture of excellence, keep focusing on the people and your process and the results will take care of themselves.

You stop looking at people for what they can do for you, and start finding out what you can do for them.

This type of leadership and teamwork is another example of what it takes to bring everyone together. You stop looking at people for what they can do for you, and start finding out what you can do for them.

People aren't just an asset. They are essential. They are humans with emotions, needs, and desires to bring value. They want to feel a sense of belonging, and that they are part of something so much bigger than themselves.

When you work to create a team that considers one another family, you will transform your culture.

chapter seventeen

MORE THAN WORDS

One of my favorite songs of the 90's is *More Than Words*, by Extreme. The melody, harmony and feelings created from the song bring back some really great memories.

You know what's even better?

The words.

The lyrics paint a beautiful picture of what it means to show people you care about them. You don't even need to speak a word when your actions say it all.

Wow.

A great reminder that your communication is one thing, your actions are the proof.

My friend, Larry Dietz, has been the General Manager for Professional Plating Inc. for nearly 20 years. Their team of a couple hundred people puts finishing touches on metal parts. During his tenure, he and the team have grown, especially over the last five years. Larry credits this growth to the team focusing on a culture change.

I have been honored to be a part of the PPI journey over the last six years. From speaking to the entire team at annual meetings, and even coaching several of their emerging leaders, I've seen this first hand.

What I have come to learn is that anyone can buy a building, buy equipment, and hire people. Anyone can have a business, have clients, and make money.

Not just anyone can sustain success, create loyalty, and be a difference maker in their community.

That takes a special type of team. A silver platter service team. A team that lives on more than words.

PPI lives by a set of cultural expectations, which includes:

- » Listen for Understanding and Learning
- » Communicate in a Positive and Respectfu Manner
- » Support and Respect Fellow Team Members
- » Applaud Others and Be Thankful
- » Follow Procedures and Accept Direction to Promote $uccess
- » Be Involved...Ask Why - Speak Up - Learn More - Share More

» Give and Share Input to Prevent Concerns and Promote Good
» Remain Positive and Receptive to a Question - Refrain from being defensive

What a list!

They are not just words, though. This is their way of working, and their way of living.

I know they don't pay the highest in their marketplace. They actually have a major corporation directly across the street who employs seven times the number of employees as PPI, and pays more money per hour.

What I also know is the PPI team believes in treating people well, with respect, keeping them safe, and giving of themselves to one another. Through that foundation, they create an amazing work environment.

It is more than pay.

It is more than words.

It is about creating a culture of excellence. Not just at PPI, but in their community as well.

See, creating a culture of excellence goes beyond your four walls. You live in a culture and a community. That culture isn't separate from you, it is created in part by you.

A main mantra at PPI recently has been:

Keep flooding good.

"Randy, I grew up in a family that made sure others had enough first. It's just who I am." Larry continued, "We wanted to do everything we could to care for others."

PPI just kept on flooding good.

They bought food for their team every week using a local company. It helped team morale, supported a local business, and is living proof of their culture in action. See the next page for a social media post from one of those lunches.

One more example I've seen from Larry and PPI is how you build trust by being transparent with plans, policies, and expectations.

They always tell the truth. They don't bend their integrity. They lead with consistency and expect it from their team.

To grow their level of trust and transparency, they had to take action (more than words) to ensure their communication was open, easy to understand and consistent.

Two years ago, they implemented an application called *Pro Connect*. Team members install the app on their smart device allowing for multiple things, including, but not limited to:

Larry Dietz · 1st
General Manager at Professional Plating Inc.
1mo · ⊗

Professional Plating Inc. is working to meet the needs of our essential customers. Our TEAM has been very supportive. We are also making sure that our local restaurant partners who are being impacted greatly during the COVID-19 situation are being supported. We have been "Buying Local" and providing free lunches to over 165 team members to thank our TEAM for their passion and support during these trying times. Thanking our TEAM and supporting our local partners so we all make it thru to the other side of this situation. Our local providers are Cobblestone Inn, Braun's at Deer Run and Markos BBQ

Post courtesy of Larry Dietz

» Leaders send mass communications to the entire PPI team
» Individual departments communicate with their team
» Safety communications are sent

- » There is an applause function where team members celebrate one another for great work
- » Individual team members can message any leader 24/7, and vice versa
- » Groups of teams can also set up group messages for specific projects

As of this writing, over 97% of the team uses the app every day. This is way beyond an "open door policy" or a monthly company newsletter.

Even though it is just a tool, this resource has become an intentional and integral part of their culture.

It builds trust. It creates efficiency in business logistics and schedules (making them more profitable) and it keeps the team together as they grow.

As Larry says, "It keeps connection cool."

My friends, you can do this too. Your team needs to see the lived out actions.

Communication is key to working effectively together.

Communication is more than memos, meetings, and mission statements on a wall.

Communication is more than being honest, being timely, and being transparent.

Oh yes, it is all of those things, but there is so much more!

To be a great team, yes, you need to be great communicators. You also need people who take initiative, use creativity, think of others, and keep flooding good.

You need to live out your culture expectations with actions. People will know who you are and what your culture is based on your actions.

And they will know it without your saying a word.

chapter eighteen

THE TURNAROUND

Jerry Roames is a great friend, trusted husband, father, and my pastor.

Jerry's journey to ministry included several retail stops along the way, including Target and Bealls Department Stores.

In speaking to him recently about his business experience, I realized one of the largest takeaways from those experiences in the world of retail and commerce is this:

The key principles that worked in retail work in other areas of life too: including personal, family, church... literally, anywhere.

Upon arriving at Bealls, Jerry quickly discovered the trouble that had been partially described by the leadership that hired him. He was brought in to help a floundering operation get back to profitability, as quickly as possible.

The numbers didn't lie, they were more than floundering. They were losing.

Big time!

Nearly $700,000 in the red in one year.

Even if you have never worked in a business, you can appreciate the tough situation. With those abysmal numbers, you don't stay in business long. No person, family, or organization can survive that amount of loss.

In order to turn around the business, he had to change the business. To change the business he had to change the culture.

Four key areas he and his team focused on included:

» Empowering everyone to make a difference
» Using best practices daily
» Being accountable for yourself and to others
» Trusting in God in all things

We will briefly touch on each of these, starting with the last area first.

This isn't a religious book, yet a real life example that prayer does work; even in professional situations, corporate settings, public education, anywhere.

Jerry started every day with prayer. At first on his own, then he would invite team members to join him.

Let's be clear. No one was ever forced to join him, it was simply an invitation. It wasn't a public prayer, it was a small gathering of people choosing to participate.

The prayers were for many things, but for one thing primarily. The key each day was for a covering of help to do their best to serve everyone the best they could. To simply meet them where they were, as people first, potential buyers second.

Interestingly enough, as the days went along, more team members voluntarily joined the opening day prayer. Silently, in most cases, yet they were present.

Jerry shared that this was the foundation of their cultural change.

Through this spiritual connection time, the team realized it wasn't all on them.

What was expected of the people, though, was the understanding that best practices must be utilized and followed each and every day. Every moment.

There could be no days off when it came to applying best practices.

Jerry and the team began to see how things would change, service would improve, and the numbers would follow in the right direction. With that, though, was the tendency for team members to relax.

As soon as something got a little better, they would rest a bit. They would relax once they thought they had made it to the pinnacle.

Maybe they thought no one would notice if the racks were a little messy, or the floor wasn't squeaky clean.

Jerry wouldn't allow that to happen.

You can't either.

He kept the pressure on.

The reminder to be their best, every day and every time.

The prayer session was for help to serve well, but it was Jerry's job to ensure that the people did their parts as well. He empowered them to create, innovate and make a difference.

This pursuit of excellence only happened with the consistent expectation that nothing but excellence was accepted.

And expected.

Best practices were implemented and expected to be followed.

And when they weren't, there were consequences.

See how quickly having best practices leads to accountability?

Jerry was at this location for less than two years. In that time, his location became the corporate headquarters' touring site.

From the cleanliness, to the staging of the product, to the amazing customer service, the store had transformed. It was first class, silver platter level service, and best in class at Bealls.

Now you may be thinking this is fluffy stuff. He worked on his culture, shot up a few prayers, asked his team to follow some procedures...and presto!

Well, it was more than presto and more than fluff. This transformation was hard work.

It was an intentional decision to make cultural transformation a necessity. See, this work goes above and beyond the daily tasks.

And that is why so many teams don't do it.

They just want to check the box, do the bare minimum, not get fired, go home, and collect a paycheck.

That is exactly how this operation found itself losing $700,000 a year.

That was before Jerry and the transformation began.

Just a short time later, this operation was making $750,000 per year.

A $1.5 million dollar turnaround in less than 18 months.

Not fluff.

Not easy.

Yet attainable.

The key is not focusing on the results or accepting substandard work. Focus on best practices and accountability.

Exchange your striving for perfection for a _continual pursuit of excellence._

The key is also not going alone.

Tap into every source you have, in your team and from above.

Realize that when you prioritize your team and your customers, with a focus on excellence, you can drastically change your trajectory.

Most importantly, keep the pressure on.

Cultural transformation is a never-ending propulsion toward excellence.

Not perfection.

Excellence.

Pursuing perfection is unattainable, it brings about

frustration and negativity. You cannot be perfect, but you and your team can be excellent.

Exchange your striving for perfection for a continual pursuit of excellence.

chapter nineteen

LEADING FROM THE TOP

I would be remiss if I didn't acknowledge that the leadership of an organization is going to be key for the culture transformation. There is no question, no denying, that everything rises and falls on leadership.

It is also important to note, and I've stated this from the platform and in other books, everyone is a leader.

Let's say that again. *Everyone is a leader.*

Why?

Everyone has influence.

Yes, I'm talking to you too.

Everyone of you reading this right now has a sphere of influence in your life. There are people that will think, act, and behave differently moving forward because of something you say or do.

Your ability to influence others is your leadership capacity. Everyone is a leader because everyone can influence by example.

Recently, my daughter received a leadership award at her school. Marne and I were very proud parents; our 8 year old was demonstrating leadership at her young age. Upon receiving this award, her teacher, the wonderful Mrs. Humphrey shared this:

"A leader is one who demonstrates, by example, how to properly act, think, and respond to many different situations; thus guiding others to do the same. A leader inspires others to greatness and strives to do his or her best through it all."

If the expectation from a teacher is for 8-year-olds to live out this type of leadership, we can absolutely expect this from adults!

You can do this, I know you can. You can lead by example.

Since everyone is a leader, and teams are made up of people, this is a basic math formula. Every team has as many leaders as there are team members.

The truth, though, is not all leaders have the same influence. Some have louder voices, some have more authority in the workplace, some just have more courage to set the example.

Over the past decade, I've had the privilege to have mentoring conversations with a very successful corporate executive. More importantly, I've been blessed to call Mark Englizian friend.

Mark spent his career in human resource management. From training and development, coaching, building systems and teams, he led very influential teams to drive results for massive corporations.

How about this for massive? Some of his stops included Walgreens, Amazon, and Microsoft. He is now coaching C Suite executives in Fortune 500 companies across the country, and advising teams and owners as a member on several boards of directors.

In a recent conversation with Mark, I gathered three distinct insights for leaders.

Do I need to remind you? Ok, I will. You are a leader.

As you look to transform, here are three things you can do.

1. Narrow Your Lane

Executives have too many direct reports. In part, it is because there is a general lack of trust and they want their hand in everything.

Mark shared, "I'm seeing a big need for executives to reduce direct reports from 10 or 12 people down to 2 - 3 people. This is more than just organizational chart changes and reporting, this is about actually trusting people. The only way this works is if leaders and team members have a verbal contract of trust.

You need people on your team that you trust. People who deliver results.

If you need more on trust, go back and reread section two of this book.

2. Have a Plan

Again, things don't just happen, it takes intentional and specific actions and plans to map out transformation. When it comes to teams, investing in your people is critical. To work effectively together, each member needs to be working at their own highest level of potential.

Here are three ways to improve individual performance:

A. Have the right people

>> Keep the best, maybe 75%, the rest are replaced with new hires
>> Find the right spots for your people

B. Invest in your team

>> Once a week, for 6 months, meet one on one with each team member

- » Create a 360 assessment tool for everyone: evaluate up, down, sideways, internally and externally
- » Once a month, host a retreat: spend the day on development, hire other speakers, share your vision on how to get better

C. Set client expectations

- » Go and speak to your clients (whether internal or external)
- » Admit where you are failing and ask how, together, you could be better
- » Outline how they could be a good client to help you make your team serve them better

Mark did this, over and over again. In the end, his teams improved performance, gained confidence, and enhanced relationships with their clients. Most of his team members became extremely marketable, and some went on to executive positions at Fortune 100 companies.

3. Lead by Example

This is a true story from one of Mark's trips, while he was an executive at Walgreens.

Mark forgot his entire personal kit: toothbrush, razor, deodorant...everything! He walked down the street from his hotel, and of course, went to Walgreens. He decided not to say anything about who he was, in effect, he became a customer and a secret shopper for his company.

As he approached the counter with all his items, the person helping him didn't say a word. She never even looked at him. No thank you, no hello.

Nothing.

The excursion to Walgreens was successful though. As for products for purchase, it wasn't horrible. Mark got what he needed, he wasn't over charged. He was able to complete the transaction.

Yet, he wasn't acknowledged as a person or a customer. Not even a glimpse of excellence or silver platter service in this situation.

This interaction bothered Mark. He was frustrated as a customer and an executive of the company. As he wrestled with the experience all night long, he finally came to a decision.

He had to do something.

The next day he went back to the same store. He walked up to a different employee, introduced himself as an executive at Walgreens, and shared the story.

"This is not the type of service we can have at Walgreens." Mark said sternly.

The employee responded, "I'm so sorry. The woman

who was working last night wasn't even supposed to be in yesterday. She had a close family member pass away and really needed time off. Unfortunately, we had someone call in sick and she was kind enough to cover. She obviously wasn't in a great place."

Ugh.

Mark's heart sinks. He – and all of us – learn this truth:

It's easy to judge others based on a small amount of information.

This occurs far too frequently in our culture today. We judge others. We cast blame. We expect something. We believe we are entitled.

If we are honest, all of us have done this at some point. We don't really do or say anything to create interaction or relationship, yet we expect it.

We expect great service, right? We are the customers. We deserve it!

Well, leaders go first. Our world is waiting for *you* to be kind. This is the moment we stop judging. *Someone has to go first.* Someone has to have courage to lead.

Is that someone you?

Mark said to me, "Randy, what if I had been more friendly *first*? That would have changed our interaction..."

Even though Mark didn't say who he was, he still was thinking and judging based on who he was in his position at the time.

And to be honest, we judge too.

Every moment with every person, regardless of where you are, is an opportunity to lead and create excellence. Every interaction is a culture transformational moment.

As you look to create a culture of excellence, it isn't just about your own team, or your own company, it is about *our* society. It is about everyone you encounter. It starts with you and it affects everything!

What will you do to be a good customer, to care for others you meet, to encourage others you see on a daily basis? It's time for you to go first.

Here are a few simple ways to lead first:

- » Say hello
- » Ask people how they are doing
- » Listen
- » Smile
- » Open a door
- » Brighten someone's day
- » Have patience
- » Forgive
- » Teach
- » And the list goes on…

See, sometimes if you want great service, you need to be the one serving. You need to be the one creating the culture.

Stop expecting the world to change, or be kind and loving.

You need to lead, first.

Leading from the top is really about leading from any chair. Of course you can select the right people, put a strategy in place to develop them, and ultimately, serve them. You can be a leader who builds teams and tackles tough times with great solutions.

You have a choice, though.

You can be the one who changes everything!

Be like, and lead like, the world; demand, direct and expect.

Or, you can be a culture transformer. You can be the one who sets the example, who serves and inspires others. Don't miss this: You can be the one who changes everything!

You can lead by serving.

Go ahead.

I dare you.

chapter twenty

YOUR CULTURE CULMINATION

I told you this isn't easy.

I also said it was worth it.

As we see from all of these amazing examples, with intentionality, you create the culture you desire.

You create the culture by doing right by your people. That creates a culture that is people-centric.

With a people-centric approach, teams work effectively together.

As they work effectively together, performance improves, engagement increases, fulfillment ensues.

People will love their jobs and who they serve.

The culture of excellence is well on the way.

Creating the culture of excellence is one thing, maintaining and growing it is another.

How do you do that?

You never settle.

You accept that the pinnacle of success is never fully reached.

You expect setbacks, and keep going!

You still celebrate milestones, appreciate people and focus on engagement. What you don't do is stop.

You continually improve through a willingness to change. You consistently build trust, and work to make each and every day a little better than the day before. Together.

You find small ways to make a big difference.

You tweak, adjust, and adapt.

You innovate in the smallest of ways, continuously.

You lead well, and you lead first.

When consistently applied as a team, with individuals contributing small silver platter moments, you make lasting, impactful impressions.

Simply put, you create a culture of excellence.

This brings us to the inspiration for this book. Of course, one more story...I'm a speaker, what did you expect?!

My wife and I had the pleasure to experience this while traveling to a speaking event.

This story shows us that anyone, and everyone, can create a culture of excellence by simply serving.

Not just any type of service.

Silver platter service.

chapter twenty-one

THE SILVER PLATTER

It was a cold, wintery, day in early December 2017
as my wife and I boarded our flight to San Antonio
from Chicago.

We were excited to take a business trip together and
enjoy some needed couple time!

Our journey begins with instructions from the flight
attendants.

I have to be honest, many flight attendants don't
seem too excited as they deliver instructions and
provide service. This, among other factors, can make
air travel not very pleasant.

We need to realize, however, that sometimes the
service level gap is massive.

We don't always get great service.

So, we have a gap and therein lies the opportunity.

Take the drink process for example. I have heard so many times, as they walk down the aisle, "Drink, drink, do you want a drink?" The sound is more of a frustrated demand than a sincere question.

I've even heard, "I can't hear you, speak up, what do you want?"

Unfortunately, it seems like they are just checking a box.

They typically walk down the aisles and offer you a beverage. What they are not required to do is be friendly, kind, or appear like you or your business matter.

Our flight was not typical. I noticed right away, our flight attendant was different. This was going to be an amazing experience.

Come, sit in our seats. Row 6, seats A and B, as we begin our Southwest Airlines flight. I invite you to sit back, relax, and enjoy your journey with...Abraham.

Here he comes from the galley. Dressed to the nines in his suit, complete with tie, vest, and a pocket handkerchief.

As he approaches row one, we hear him say, "What could I have the pleasure of bringing you today?" The passenger replies with "Coffee, one cream."

He smiles and replies, "That sounds so good, if that

seat was open next to you I'd sit down and join you with my own cup."

Wow.

Row by row we hear him remarking, complimenting and thanking his clients that day for joining him for the flight.

Oooh...here we go, he is now arriving at row 6. It's our turn.

What will he say?

Certainly he has either run out of nice one liners or we will get the second class treatment.

"Well, hello my friends, so glad to see you! Now sir," as he looks me in the eye, "I would be no gentleman if I didn't ask the lovely, and beautiful, woman sitting next to you what she wanted first."

Thank goodness he is referring to my wife! Marne beams from his chivalry and sincere remarks.

Not only did Abraham make her feel special, he made me look good too.

Marne and I look at one another, our eyes say it all. This airline may not have a first class section, but this sure felt like first class service!

Now it's time to collect the garbage. Let's leave our flight momentarily to check in on a lesser experience on another flight.

The typical experience is of flight attendants opening up a big, plastic garbage bag. They put on plastic gloves and head down the aisles.

You would hear, "Trash, trash, trash."

They literally look right at you and call you trash!

To be fair, this process does the job. The bag collects the garbage, the gloves keep their hands fairly clean, etc.

It is adequate, and it is efficient.

We expect this.

We accept this.

What we don't do is rave about it. We aren't moved by it.

It does nothing to provide us with an experience of excellence.

Back to our flight with Abraham.

He has a heart to serve, with excellence. With *silver platter service* excellence. We know from how he offered drinks that his collection process must be something to behold.

And we were right.

Keep your eyes and ears open as we learn how Abraham, and you too, can take a mundane task and turn it into a silver platter service experience.

Literally.

Abraham comes out of the galley, still in full suit, no apron, no gloves, no garbage bag.

He approaches row one to collect their trash with a shiny, empty silver platter!

After he has completed row one, he walks back to the galley, empties the platter, and returns to row two. Again, with a shiny silver platter.

He repeats this process, and comes back again, to each row, collecting trash with the silver platter. He gets to us. Are you ready?

The first thing we do is look down at the silver platter. All we can see is the reflection of the smile on his face.

He politely asks me, "Sir, are you done?"

"I am," I said.

"May I take this?

"Yes you may," I reply.

And his response, "You're too kind."

I was too kind to give him my trash on a silver platter!

My friends, this is collecting garbage, with a powerful learning for us all.

Any of us, you, me, anyone can serve others in this manner. There are a myriad of tasks, projects, or responsibilities that with a slight tweak can become awesome!

What can you do...no…what *will* you do to create this type of moment for your team, your client, your family, and your community?

When I say "The world is waiting for you!" this is what I'm talking about.

The world is starving for this type of love and servant leadership.

Why do you think Abraham decided to take the time and effort to do this? Why take something so simple as garbage collection and turn it into an elegant, silver platter experience?

We don't need to guess or theorize, I spoke to him and he gave us his answer.

Later in our flight I walked up front, introduced myself, and asked him about his service levels.

I wanted to know the *why* behind his actions.

Being a frequent flyer on Southwest, I have come to learn about their culture. I understand their Luv logo, how people matter most to them, how they empower employees, and go above and beyond for their clients and community.

Yet, with that, I still had never experienced anything like Abraham. Before, or since.

As we continued to chat, I said, "You really seem to love your job, Abraham."

"I do love my job, Mr. Fox."

Notice "Randy" wasn't sufficient for him.

"You know what, though" he continued, "my job is such a pleasure and I'm truly grateful for you being with us today. The real thing for me, I simply *love* people and seeing them smile."

That was it.

The bottom line and core element to silver platter service.

Love.

A pure, real, heartfelt love for people.

Love.

Seen in action, and driven from the heart.

This love isn't about money, education, social status, or all of the other worldly things we can materially attain.

We can all do this.

You can do this.

You can serve well and have a team with a culture of excellence *because you can love people*.

You can serve well and have a team with a culture of excellence because you can love people.

In order for your service levels to be high, and your culture to consistently transform closer to excellence, you need to love people.

Truly love people.

Maybe this is hard to do because our world doesn't seem to even know what real love is.

So, if you don't mind, as we close out this book, may I provide for you a guide as to what it means to truly love.

chapter twenty-two

LOVING WELL

Those that offer silver platter service and build cultures of excellence simply know how to love others. And they know how to love others well.

The items below are based on a passage you may have heard at a wedding or two. It is found in what is called by so many, the love chapter, from 1 Corinthians 13:4-8.

People who love well are:

Patient: Life isn't about what you want when you want it. Easier said than done. Breathe. Remain patient.

Kind: Not just nice, kind. Sharing what people *need* to hear, not what they want to hear.

Yet, your words are filled with love, always kind and gentle.

Not Envious: Your chance to cheer others on, no matter what. Even when you lose, you are happy when others succeed.

Encouraging: Always building others up, never tearing people down. Always thinking of others' interests and needs, not just your own.

Humble: Admitting you aren't always right. Furthermore, not boasting or being so prideful as to say, "Look at me!" Or as my grandpa would say, "Never toot your own horn."

Honoring: This is different from respect. Respect is earned, but honor is given. You simply choose to honor people. Not based on what they did, just because of who they are.

People-centric People: Being driven for goals for others, the team, the family and the community before seeking things for yourself.

Self Controlled: Remaining calm in tough situations, not getting too easily angered. Self control means to listen first, pause a moment, and then speak.

Forgiving: Real love means to completely forgive, no matter what. Keeping score and bringing up the past is never done. We all make mistakes. Learn to forgive and move forward.

Rejoicers of Truth: Not even a hint of a white lie, or little cover up in your bones. Trustworthy, truthful, full of integrity, period. Don't be a deal breaker, be the deal maker. Truth wins and brings joy!

Protectors: You love so well you protect the life of others. "Greater love has no one than this: to lay down one's life for one's friends." *John 15:13 NIV*

Constantly Hopeful: For some people the glass is half full, some it's half empty. How about living as if it's always being filled and is overflowing? There is hope, there is always hope. You are still here to make a difference.

Persistent: Relationships are hard, life is hard, but with persistence, love wins. Teams win. Relationships built on love continue to get stronger. Teams built on love work effectively together. Communities and families filled with love never quit. They win.

Why? Because love never fails.

Love wins.

Excellence is created and service levels improve when we love.

Bottom line results improve when we love.

Our world is better when we love.

Okay, truth telling time.

As I wrote the above list, I reflected on how challenging it is for me to live this out. There is no question I miss the mark on several of these every day. I simply don't get it right in every interaction. Using this as my guide, however, I continue the *pursuit* of excellence.

Remember, we aren't aiming for perfection, the pursuit is for excellence.

By making the pursuit of excellence a mantra by which you live, you will make a difference in the world.

You will deliver silver platter service.

You will help your team create a culture of excellence.

Trust me.

This is the list to live, work, and set your compass by.

Now, make no mistake, this is difficult. As we said in the beginning, this process starts with a decision.

By making the pursuit of excellence a mantra by which you live, you will make a difference in the world.

You must simply decide it is important enough to do.

You must decide the journey is worth it.

You need to be willing to change, to grow...to be better.

You need to be a change agent, build trust, and keep your team, your family, and your community working effectively together.

You need to serve.

You can do this!

Never give up!

I believe in you!

Go out, show the world some love.

Give them silver platter service.

Commit to creating a culture of excellence everywhere you go.

And never forget.

No matter where you go, what you do, or who you meet:

The world is waiting for YOU!

-Randy

ACKNOWLEDGEMENTS

Writing this book has been such a rewarding experience. I learned so much about people and, more importantly, how much we really have in common. This idea of coming together to change our culture and pursue excellence is exactly what happened for this book to come to fruition.

God has blessed me with an amazing wife in Marne. I choose you, and thank you for choosing me. We have three wonderful children, two of which are now grown men, one with a family of his own. I am grateful for our entire Fox Family and the life we have together.

Thank you to my creative team, who put talent, ideas, time and heart into this book. Appreciate you Aurelie for the cover design and Trevor for the layout and marketing. Thank you Marne, Aurelie, Ken and my mom for the fabulous edits, you make my words easier to read.

To all the great friends and clients who shared stories, thought leadership and your passion to help others, thank you. So grateful for April, Jerry, Larry, Mark, Rachel and Tim. Dub, thank you for your support and writing the perfect foreword.

Thanks to the countless people that have supported me personally, the FoxPoint business and our family. Thank you for adding value to my life and to this project.

If you are still reading this, thank you. You are why I do this.

I consider it an honor to be a part of your journey. Thank you for allowing me in as part of your team and your life.

Looking forward to the future…together!

ABOUT THE AUTHOR

Silver Platter Service is the sixth book on leadership from award-winning keynote speaker and professional development coach Randy Fox.

As the Founder of FoxPoint, Randy's mission is to use his God-given abilities to help people transform their professional and personal lives. He earned his stripes with 23 years as an NCAA basketball official and 20 years filled with much success (and some failure too) as a corporate operations and sales leader.

Randy and his wife Marne live in Central Florida. They have three wonderful children, two of which are now grown men, one with a family of his own. Randy loves serving, leading, and living life with the entire Fox Family.

OTHER BOOKS FROM RANDY FOX

Explore life lessons learned on and off the court. Learn how to enjoy the great game of life by showing up, playing the game, and discovering the lessons and principles that will help you along the way.

Discover the 9 strategies every winning team adapts, implements, and executes to find and sustain their victory!

A Leader Worth Following is for those that believe in vision, character, appreciation, serving others and much more. We need authentic, trustworthy, competent men and women - this journey starts with you!

KEYNOTE EXPERIENCES

Randy's incredible energy, leadership expertise, and undeniable stage charisma all come together to engage your audience, maximize their potential, expand their leadership influence and motivate them to pursue excellence!

Similar to the way he writes, Randy speaks with a blend of powerful storytelling, charisma, and humor. And no podiums, PowerPoints, or handouts!

To explore Randy's existing keynotes or learn about how he can tailor a message for your team, visit **www.foxpoint.net/keynotes** or email Randy at **randy@foxpoint.net.**

"Nothing short of fantastic, inspiring and on point!"
- BIC Corporation